CONTENTS

Special thanks to all the children and adults who tested the crafts and gave us their valuable comments:

Becky and Carrie Albrecht and their mother Nancy Albrecht
Selena Amundson and her mother Nancy Amundson
Alexandra Bartol and her mother Lori Bartol
Erin Becker and her mother Carol Becker
Kala and Megan Bergin and their mother Betsy Bergin
Jessica Blanchard and her mother Deanna Blanchard
Molly Brosius and her mother Mary Brosius
Heather Bybee and her mother Kelly Bybee
Alanna Clarke and her mother Mary Anne Clarke
Clarin Collins and her mother Ellie Collins
Anna-Lisa Dahlgren and her mother Donna Dahlgren
Rose Dauck and her mother Linda Dauck
Samantha Davis and her mother Debra Davis
Jenny Diebold and her mother Virginia Diebold
Genieve Dodsworth and her mother Beth Dodsworth
Amanda Doruff and her mother Sharon Doruff
Bailey Drake and her mother Rita Bardell
Katie and Emily Duesler and their mother Diane Duesler
Alli Dumphy and her mother Jill Dumphy
Sarah Eastman and her mother Wendy Eastman
Amanda Eaton and her mother Ann Eaton
Sarah Eklund and her mother Sandy Eklund
Kai Ellestad and her mother Marty Ellestad
Catherine Enderlin and her mother Caroline Enderlin
Heather and Michelle Ervasti and their mother Julie Ervasti
Morgan and Page Evans and their mother Jane Evans
Lauren and Lisa Fahey and their mother Deb Fahey
Ashley Farmer and her mother Cheryl Farmer
Kacia Ferguson and her mother Spring Sherrod
Anna, Eleanor, and Leah Fink and their mother Marcia Fink
Meaghan Finneke and her mother Mary Finneke
Maria Frigo and her mother Stella Frigo
Julie Fischmann and her mother Cathy Fischmann
Julia Gustafson and her mother Cynthia Gustafson
Caitlin Johnson and her mother LaVonne Johnson
Jessica Stringer and her mother Peggy Stringer
Emily Tupper and her mother Cricket Tupper

And thanks to our focus group testers:
Madeleine Calhoun, Lauryn Durtschi, Samuel Fullerton,
Joel Meyer-England, Heather Preston, and Kaeli and Lindsay Urben.

1824

JOSEFINA'S CRAFT BOOK

*A Look at
Crafts from the
Past with Projects
You Can Make Today*

PLEASANT COMPANY PUBLICATIONS

Published by Pleasant Company Publications

Printed in the United States of America.
98 99 00 01 02 03 WCR 10 9 8 7 6 5 4 3 2 1

PICTURE CREDITS
The following individuals and organizations have generously
given permission to reprint images in this book:
1—Alexander Harmer, History Collections, Los Angeles County Museum of Natural
History; 4—Jack Parsons Photography; 6—Cómoda del comedor de la hacienda del Jaral
de Berrio, Santa María del Rio, Fondo Cultural Bancen; 7—Jack Parsons Photography;
13—Photography by Michel Zabe (top); Jack Parsons Photography (bottom);
17—ECHEVERRIA, Beatriz, Johann Moritz Rugendas. Colección Museo Nacional de
Historia CNCA–INAH, Mexico City. 19—Fred Harvey Collection of the International
Folk Art Foundation Collections at the Museum of International Folk Art, Museum of
New Mexico, Santa Fe. Photo by Cradoc Bagshaw (top); Photo by Blair Clark (bottom);
21—Museum of Indian Arts & Culture/Laboratory of Anthropology, Santa Fe, cat.
#42247/12. Photo by Blair Clark (left); The Field Museum, neg. #A109998c; 27—The Field
Museum, neg. #A113497c, cat. #8400; 30—Poblanas en Santa Fe, Johann Moritz Rugendas.
Colección Museo Nacional de Historia CNCA–INAH, Mexico City. Photography by
Michel Zabé; 31—Jack Parsons Photography; 33—Museo Franz Mayer, Mexico City;
36—Courtesy of Domitila and George Villa; 37—International Folk Art Foundation
Collections at the Museum of International Folk Art, Santa Fe. Photo by Blair Clark;
39—Courtesy Mondadori; 41—Private collection; 44—Edward S. Curtis, Museum of New
Mexico, neg. #31961; Don Pedro de Peralta surveying the site for Santa Fe in 1610.
Painting by Roy Grinnell. Courtesy Sunwest Bank of Santa Fe and Roy Grinnell.

Written and Edited by Tamara England
Designed and Art Directed by Pat Tuchscherer and Jane S. Varda
Produced by Cheryll Mellenthin and Anne Ruh
Cover Illustration by Mike Wimmer
Inside Illustrations by Geri Strigenz Bourget
Photography by Mark Salisbury and Jamie Young
Historical and Picture Research by Rebecca Sample Bernstein,
Kathy Borkowski, Tamara England, and Debra Shapiro
Crafts Made by Jean doPico, Tamara England, Virginia Gunderson
Sarajane Lien, and June Pratt
Craft Testing Coordinated by Jean doPico
Prop Research by Jean doPico

Special thanks to Sandra Jaramillo, Tey Diana Rebolledo, Orlando Romero,
and Marc Simmons for their review of the manuscript.

Library of Congress Cataloging-in-Publication Data

Josefina's craft book : a look at crafts from the past with projects you can make today /
[written and edited by Tamara England ; inside illustration by Geri Strigenz Bourget ;
photography by Mark Salisbury]. — 1st ed.
p.   cm.—(The American girls collection)
Summary: Provides information about life on a ranch in nineteenth century
New Mexico and instructions for a variety of related craft projects.
ISBN 1-56247-670-X (softcover)
1. Handicraft—Juvenile literature. 2. New Mexico—Social life and customs—
19th century—Juvenile literature. [1. Handicraft.
2. New Mexico—Social life and customs—19th century.]
I. England, Tamara. II. Bourget, Geri Strigenz, ill.
III. Salisbury, Mark, ill. IV. Series.
TT171.J67   1998   745.5'09791'0903—dc21   98-4752   CIP   AC

CRAFTS FROM THE PAST

During the 1820s, life on a northern New Mexico *rancho*, or farm, was busy from morning till night. Josefina and her sisters rose with the sun to early morning chores. Their days followed the steady rhythm of the family's work on the rancho.

A woman sewing outdoors.

Girls like Josefina helped their mothers, grandmothers, and aunts with sewing, weaving, gardening, and cooking. There wasn't a lot of time to play, and the few toys they had were usually handmade. Children took good care of their playthings so they would last a long time. Some toys, like Niña, the doll Mamá had made, were passed from one child to the next.

But rancho children were resourceful. Girls used their sewing skills to make beautiful things to wear. They made toys and created games from things they found around the rancho—dried grasses and cornhusks from the fields, clay from the earth, and scraps from the sewing basket. Children like Josefina made practical things, too, such as frames for mirrors and moccasins for everyday wear.

Learning how and why crafts were made long ago will help you understand what it was like to grow up the way Josefina did. Making the crafts she might have made will bring history alive for you today.

JOSEFINA ❀ 1824

María Josefina Montoya grew up in northern New Mexico when it was still part of Mexico. She and her sisters learned to sew and weave when they were very young. They used their skills to make practical things for their home and playthings for fun.

●

Remember that in Spanish, "j" is pronounced like "h." That means that Josefina's name is pronounced "ho-seh-FEE-nah."

You'll find some Spanish words in this book. Use the glossary on page 44 to see what a word means and how to pronounce it.

CRAFT TIPS

This list of tips gives you some hints about creating the crafts in this book. But this is the most important tip: **work with an adult**. The best thing about these crafts is the fun you will have making them together.

1. Choose a time that suits you and the adult who's working with you, so that you will both enjoy making crafts together.

2. You can find most of the materials listed in this book in your home or at craft and fabric stores. If an item in the materials list is starred (*), look at the bottom of the list to find out where you can get it.

3. If you don't have something you need or can't find it at the store, think of something similar you could use. You might just think of something that works even better!

4. Read the instructions for a craft all the way through before you start it. Look at the pictures. They will help you understand the steps.

5. If there's a step that doesn't make sense to you, try it out with a piece of scrap paper or fabric first. Sometimes acting it out helps.

6. Select a good work area for your craft project. Pick a place that has plenty of light and is out of reach of pets and younger brothers and sisters.

PAINTS AND BRUSHES

You'll use water-based, or **acrylic**, *paints to make some of the crafts in this book. Here are a few hints for using paints and brushes:*

❋ *Don't dip your brush into the paint bottle. Squeeze a little paint onto newspaper or a paper plate.*

❋ *Have a bowl of water handy to clean the brush each time you change colors.*

❋ *Make sure one color is dry before adding another.*

❋ *Clean your brush with soap and water and let it dry before you put it away.*

7. Wear an apron, tie back your hair, and roll up your sleeves. Cover your work area with newspapers and gather all the materials you will need before you start.

8. It pays to be careful. Be sure to get an adult's help when the instructions tell you to. Have an adult help you use tools properly. Don't use the stove or oven without an adult's permission.

9. Pay attention when using sharp knives and scissors so you don't cut your fingers! Remember—good, sharp knives and scissors are safer and easier to use than dull ones.

10. To prevent spills, put the covers back on containers tightly. If you do spill, clean it up right away.

11. If your craft doesn't turn out exactly like the picture in the book, that's terrific! The pictures are there just to give you ideas. Crafts become more meaningful when you add your own personal touch.

12. Cleanup is part of making crafts, too. Leave your work area as clean as you found it. Wash and dry dishes, trays, and tabletops. Sweep the floor. Throw away the garbage.

THREADING A NEEDLE

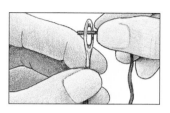

1. Wet the tip of the thread in your mouth. Then push the tip of the thread through the eye of the needle.

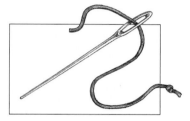

2. Pull about 5 inches of the thread through the needle. Then tie a double knot near the end of the long tail of thread.

AROUND THE RANCHO

The Montoyas got most of the things they needed from the land around their rancho. They used earth and straw to make bricks and mud plaster for the walls of their home. Corn and wheat from the rancho's fields provided food for the family, workers, and servants. And Josefina and her sisters often walked into the hills above the rancho to collect *piñón* nuts to eat and trade, and plants to make into dyes for wool and paint.

Some days, after the *siesta*, or afternoon rest, Josefina and her sisters made things with the materials they found around the rancho. Josefina liked making things that reflected the beauty of the rancho. She admired a beautiful inlaid wood chest in the family *sala,* so she decorated a small box to make it look inlaid, as she had seen craftsmen do. First, she painted a wooden box with black paint she had made by mixing soot and pine sap. Then she carefully pasted, or *appliquéd*, bits of golden grasses and dried cornhusks on the top and sides.

Josefina and her sisters made paint in other colors, too. Goldenrod made yellow paint, and insects that lived on the prickly pear cactus made red paint. The girls used the paints to decorate a wooden frame for a mirror to hang in the family sala and a wooden lantern Papá had made.

Josefina and her sisters made their own brooms, or *escobas*, from tall grasses they gathered and dried. Josefina held a bundle of stiff grasses tight in her hands while Clara tied it with a leather cord. After Josefina trimmed the grasses so the ends were even, she dipped the tip of the escoba in water and swept the dried-earth floors to "lay the dust." Josefina and Clara also gathered shorter grasses into small bundles and made hairbrushes, or *escobetillas.*

AROUND THE RANCHO

Appliquéd Treasure Box

•

Painted Frame

•

Lantern

•

Straw Broom

THE RANCHO

Josefina and her family lived on a rancho about 15 miles south of Santa Fe, the capital of New Mexico. The rancho house had thick **adobe** *walls made of mud bricks and plaster. The Montoyas grew crops such as corn, wheat, and* **chiles,** *and they raised sheep and goats. Because their rancho was far from any large town, they worked hard to get what they needed from the land around them.*

APPLIQUÉD TREASURE BOX

This box is the perfect place to store your treasures.

MATERIALS

Fine sandpaper *(150 grit)*
Unfinished wooden box with lid, 4 by 6 inches
2 foam paintbrushes, 1 inch wide
Acrylic paint *(red and black)*
Artist's paintbrush
Pencil
Piece of tracing paper, 4 by 6 inches
Scissors
1 or 2 dried cornhusks*
Straw *(oats, wheat, or any dried grasses)*
White glue *(Elmer's and Mod Podge Gloss-Lustré* are two brands.)*
Small bowl
Tweezers *(optional)*
* *Available at craft shops.*

MARQUETRY

Marquetry *(MAHR-keh-tree) is a style of decorated furniture that was popular in Josefina's time in Spain, Europe, and the Middle East. Pieces of wood, ivory, or other materials were laid into the carved surface to create elaborate patterns.*

DIRECTIONS

1. Lightly sand the wooden box and lid. Wipe away the dust.

2. Use 1 of the foam paintbrushes to paint the inside of the box red. Rinse the paintbrush. Leave the box open while paint dries.

3. When the inside is completely dry, close the box and use the foam paintbrush to paint the outside of the box black. Use the artist's paintbrush to paint around the hinges (or remove them for painting). Let the paint dry for 15 minutes. Add a second coat if necessary.

4. Open the box and paint the inside edge of the box black. Leave the box open and let it dry for at least 15 minutes. Add a second coat if necessary. Rinse the paintbrush.

5. While the paint dries, plan your box decoration. Use the design on page 43 if you like. Trace it onto tracing paper and cut it out.

6. Cut the cornhusks and straw to fit your designs. Practice laying out all the pieces on the box to create a design you like. Moving the pieces with tweezers can help.

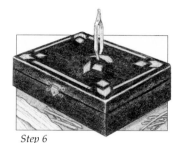

Step 6

7. When your design is settled, move the pieces off the box. Try to keep them in the pattern you've made.

8. Squeeze glue into the small bowl until it is about ¼ inch deep. Dip the other foam paintbrush into the glue.

9. Lightly brush the top of the box with an even layer of glue. The glue will look milky at first, but it will dry clear. Place the straw and cornhusk pieces on the wet box. You might need a drop of glue on the back of each piece as you apply it. Press gently to flatten the pieces.

Step 9

10. Let the glue dry for about 15 minutes. Then give the top of the box another coat of glue to seal the decorations in place. Let the glue dry.

11. When the top is dry, repeat steps 9 and 10 on the front and sides of the box, until the entire box is decorated. Be careful not to glue the lid closed.

STRAW APPLIQUÉ

*New Mexican carpenters and craftspeople were inspired by the beauty of marquetry. But instead of using wood, ivory, or shell inlays, they **appliquéd** (ap-lee-KAYD), or pasted on, inexpensive and easy-to-get materials such as cornhusks, straw, and grass. Wooden boxes, chests, and crosses were all decorated this way.*

12. To give a final seal to the box, brush one last coat of glue over all the surfaces. Again, be careful not to glue the lid closed! ✿

PAINTED FRAME

In Josefina's time, painted frames were used for mirrors and pictures of saints.

MATERIALS

Fine sandpaper *(150 grit)*
Unfinished wooden picture or craft frame,
   for a 4-by-5-inch picture
Foam paintbrush, 1 inch wide
Acrylic paints *(blue-green, white, black, and red)*
Ruler
Pencil
Small artist's paintbrush
Thick hand towel
Picture hanger*
Hammer
Mirror, 4 by 5 inches*
Putty knife or screwdriver
4 glazing points*

Available in craft shops, framing shops, or hardware stores.
Mirrors are also available in glass stores.

DIRECTIONS

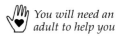 *You will need an adult to help you*

1. Lightly sand the wooden frame. Wipe away the dust. Use the foam paintbrush to paint the front and edges of the frame with the blue-green paint. Rinse the paintbrush.

2. Set the frame aside to dry for at least 15 minutes. After the paint is dry, add a second coat if necessary. Let it dry again.

3. Beginning at 1 corner, measure 1¼ inches down from the top edge. Draw a light pencil line across the frame at this point. Do the same from the side edge. Repeat for all 4 corners.

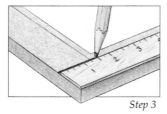

Step 3

4. Use the foam paintbrush to paint the corners white, staying within the lines you drew. After the paint is dry, add a second coat of white paint, if necessary.

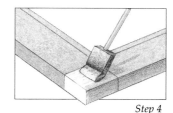
Step 4

5. When the white paint is dry, finish your frame by painting designs in black and red with the small artist's paintbrush. Let your designs dry for at least 20 minutes.

6. Decide where the top of the frame is and lay the frame facedown on the folded towel. Attach a picture hanger to the top back of the frame by gently tapping it into place with the hammer.

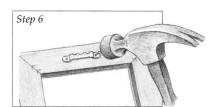
Step 6

7. Clean the mirror to remove fingerprints and smudge marks. Gently place the mirror in the frame.

8. Secure the mirror in place by using the hammer and a putty knife or screwdriver to gently tap the 4 glazing points around the inside edge of the frame, 1 on each side. ✳

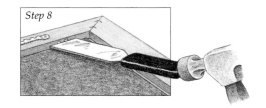
Step 8

REFLECTING LIGHT

In New Mexico in the 1820s, mirrors were used mainly to reflect light rather than to reflect a person's image. Mirrors were placed high on the wall to reflect light from candles set in **arañas** *that hung from the ceiling. American traders wrote of their surprise at seeing mirrors placed so high on the walls of Santa Fe homes.*

LANTERN

Put a small flashlight inside this lantern for soft, glowing light.

MATERIALS

Shoe box or other rectangular box with attached lid*
Pencil
Ruler
X-acto knife or scissors
Foam paintbrush, 1 inch wide
Acrylic paints, 3 or 4 colors *(including tan or light brown)*
Small artist's paintbrush
White glue
4 squares of cellophane, each 4 inches square *(light color)*
4 leather thongs: 1 thong 18 inches long, and 3 thongs
   8 inches long
Available at craft shops.

DIRECTIONS

You will need an adult to help you

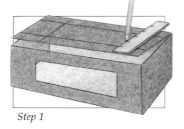

Step 1

1. On the lid and the 3 long sides of the box, measure and draw lines 4 inches from the top and bottom and 1 inch in from each side. Connect the lines and then cut out the window squares.

2. Use a foam brush to paint the outside of the box tan or brown. Let it dry. Use an artist's brush to decorate the front and sides.

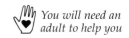

Step 3

3. Open the box. Inside, run a thin line of glue around each window. Gently place 1 cellophane square over each window and pat into place.

Step 4

4. Cut holes in the top, front, and sides of the box for a handle, 2 hinges, and a door fastener. Thread the thongs through and knot them. The longest thong is for the handle at the top of the box. ✽

STRAW BROOM

MATERIALS

Several bunches of stiff dried grasses, at least 3 feet long*
Scissors
Leather thong, 12 inches long
*Available at craft shops.

DIRECTIONS

1. Use the scissors to cut the heads off the grasses, if necessary.

2. Gather the dried grasses or straw together into a bundle that fits into one hand. The bundle should be just big enough to fill a circle formed with your thumb and index finger. Tap both ends of the bundle on the table to make them as even as possible.

Sweep your kitchen floor just as Josefina swept hers.

3. Ask a helper to hold the bundle together securely while you wrap the leather thong several times tightly around the middle of the bundle. Tie the thong in a double knot.

Step 3

4. After the broom is tied, trim the ends with the scissors to make them even.

5. To use the broom, hold it at the leather thong. As you sweep, use your fingers to fan out the straw below the thong so that the straw has a broader bottom, like brooms today. A person sweeping with this kind of broom usually has to bend over to sweep the floor! ❈

ESCOBETILLAS

New Mexican women and girls also made hairbrushes, or escobetillas. To make one for yourself, use short straw or grasses about 7 inches long.

11

SPANISH AND MEXICAN TRADITIONS

*The **Camino Real** connected New Mexico
with the rest of Mexico.*

Hundreds of years before Josefina's time, settlers from Spain and Mexico came to New Mexico, where they claimed land and built homes. Families like the Montoyas were related to those early settlers. Many of their traditions and customs were Spanish and Mexican, and families like the Montoyas enjoyed Spanish and Mexican goods, music, dances, and foods.

Like many New Mexican women and girls, Josefina and her sisters admired Spanish and European fashions. The latest styles crossed the

Atlantic Ocean to Mexico City and then traveled up the Camino Real to New Mexico. When Tía Dolores arrived from Mexico City, she brought her sewing diary filled with sketches of the latest fashions. Josefina and her sisters eagerly copied them, using goods Abuelito brought on his caravan, such as fine fabrics, laces, fringes, and trims imported from Spain, Europe, and the Far East.

New Mexican girls and women also admired the beautiful jewelry and decorated tortoiseshell hair combs that came from Spain and Mexico. But such things were expensive and hard to get, so resourceful New Mexicans made their own. When Abuelito brought Josefina and her sisters glass beads from Mexico City, they made necklaces by stringing the beads on thin leather cords. And Papá helped them make hair combs out of animal horn treated with acid and other materials so it looked like tortoiseshell.

New Mexicans also looked to Spain and Mexico in decorating their homes. Families lucky enough to have hand-tooled leather chairs, trunks, and other goods from Spain or Mexico cherished them for their beauty and craftsmanship and as links to their past.

Decorated leather chests from Mexico.

SPANISH AND MEXICAN TRADITIONS

❇

Fringed Shawl

•

Glass-Bead Necklace

•

Decorated Hair Comb

•

Stamped Leather Bookmark

FRINGED SHAWL

Josefina enjoyed carrying Mamá's fan when she wore her shawl trimmed with shimmery fringe.

MATERIALS

1½ yards of lace fabric, 45 inches wide
Iron
Scissors
Straight pins
Fringe trim, 3 yards *(in a matching or contrasting color)*
Ruler or tape measure
Thread to match the fringe trim
Needle

DIRECTIONS

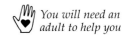
You will need an adult to help you

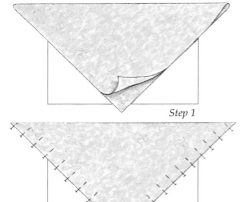
Step 1

Step 2

1. Fold the fabric into a triangle, with the *wrong side*, or back side, of the fabric folded to the inside. Ask an adult to iron out the wrinkles and press the fold.

2. Lay the fabric on a table or on the floor, and carefully line up the *raw*, or cut, edges. Use the scissors to trim the edges if they are uneven. Pin the edges together.

3. Lay the fringe trim along the 2 pinned sides, bending it at the point. If your trim comes with reinforced stitching to keep the fringe in place, do not remove the stitching until you are completely finished making your shawl.

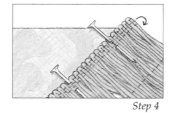
Step 4

4. Pin the fringe to the fabric, about ½ inch from the edge of the fabric. Start at 1 of the folded corners. Fold and pin about ¼ inch of the trim over the corner of the fabric.

5. Continue pinning the trim to the fabric every 1 to 2 inches. At the bottom point of the triangle, gently curve the trim around the point and continue pinning along the other side of the triangle. Do not stretch the trim. It will cause the fabric to pucker.

Step 5

6. When you reach the end of the second side of your shawl, finish by folding about ¼ inch of the trim over the corner of the shawl. Pin it in place. Cut off any extra trim.

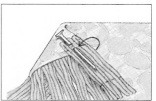

Step 6

7. Cut an 18-inch piece of thread, and thread the needle. Tie a double knot near the other end of the thread.

8. Starting at 1 end of the trim, sew the trim to the fabric with a running stitch. To sew running stitches, come up at A and go down at B.

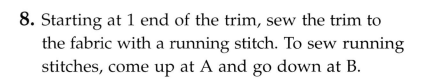

Step 8

9. Then come up at C and go down at D. When you reach the end of your thread, tie a knot close to your last stitch and cut off the extra thread. Re-thread your needle and keep stitching until you have stitched along both sides. Make smaller stitches at the corners.

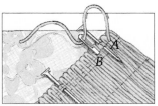

Step 9

10. Continue until you have stitched along the entire length of the trim. Remove the pins.

11. If your fringe has reinforced stitching, gently remove the line of stitching from the fringe. ✳

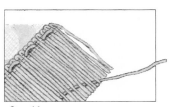

Step 11

GLASS-BEAD NECKLACE

Josefina felt very grown-up wearing her glass-bead necklace.

MATERIALS

Glass beads*, medium-size *(30–50, or enough to go ¾ of the way around your neck)*

Thin leather cord or thread, about 30 inches long

**Available at bead and craft shops.*

DIRECTIONS

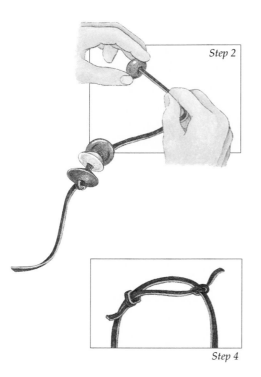

Step 2

Step 4

1. Lay the beads out and decide how you want them arranged before you start to string them.

2. Tie a loose knot about 6 inches from 1 end of the cord. String the first bead onto the cord and pull it to the knotted end.

3. String the rest of the beads onto the cord. Stop stringing beads when there are about 6 inches of cord left, or when the beads go most of the way around your neck. Untie the knot.

4. To make the necklace adjustable in length and easy to put on and take off, tie each end of the cord in a single knot around the other end of the cord. Don't tie the knots too tight, or they won't slide along the cord.

5. When both knots are tied, you'll be able to adjust the necklace to pull it over your head and then shorten it around your neck. ✳

DECORATED HAIR COMB

MATERIALS

Large hair comb
Artist's paintbrush
Acrylic paints, any colors
Beads, shells, buttons, or other decorative items *(optional)*
White glue *(optional)*

Decorated hair combs and barrettes
make great gifts!

DIRECTIONS

1. Decide on a pattern or design for your hair
comb. If you are going to add beads or shells,
lay them out first and plan where you will put
them on the comb.

2. Use the artist's paintbrush to paint your pattern
on the hair comb. Rinse and dry the brush each
time you change colors.

Step 2

3. If you are adding decorative items, wait until
the paint dries completely. Then squeeze a
small dot of glue on the back of a bead or
another decoration, and gently place it where
you want it on the hair comb. Add as many
decorative items as you like, but let the glue
dry completely before creating layers. ✤

HAIR ORNAMENTS

Hair combs from Spain and southern
Mexico were prized by New Mexican
women for their beauty and usefulness.
Women wore hair combs to hold their
hair back and to hold lace **mantillas**,
or veils, in place over their head and
shoulders.

STAMPED LEATHER BOOKMARK

Mark your place in your favorite book with a handsome hand-stamped bookmark.

MATERIALS

Sponge
Small bowl of water
Scrap of tooling leather for practice*
Piece of tooling leather, about 1½ inches wide and
   8 inches long*
Smooth flat board, slightly larger than the leather
2 or 3 leather-craft stamping tools*
Small wooden mallet*
*Available at leather-supply stores and craft shops. Look under
"Leather Supplies" in the yellow pages of the phone book.*

DIRECTIONS

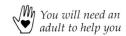 *You will need an adult to help you*

1. Dip the sponge into the bowl of water. Squeeze out some of the water.

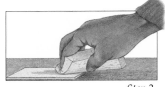
Step 2

2. First, practice on the scrap leather. Use the sponge to dampen first the rough side of the scrap leather, and then the smooth side. Dampen the piece evenly, but do not soak the leather.

3. Lay the scrap leather, rough side down, on the smooth board on a sturdy table or workbench.

4. Try out your stamping tools on the scrap leather. Hold a tool upright, with the design end resting on the leather.

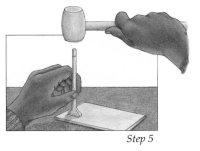
Step 5

5. Ask an adult to help you hit the stamping tool with the mallet. A firm tap is usually enough for small stamping tools. You may need to tap a few times when you use a large stamping tool.

6. When you feel comfortable stamping, plan your design. To make the design shown on the bookmark on page 18, use stamping tools numbers V400, P234, and S724.

7. When you're happy with your design, use the sponge to dampen the bookmark leather. Rub the sponge evenly over first the rough side, and then the smooth side.

8. Stamp the design onto the leather bookmark, using the technique you've practiced.

9. If the leather gets too dry, dampen it again and continue stamping until your design is finished.

10. Let the bookmark dry completely, then use it to mark your place in a good book! ✳

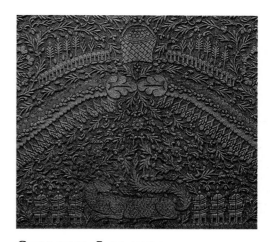

STAMPED LEATHER

This close-up of hand-stamped leather shows the elaborate design and beautiful craftsmanship valued by New Mexicans.

DECORATED LEATHER

*New Mexicans admired things that were both beautiful and useful. This Mexican saddle has distinctive **tooled**, or stamped, patterns and practical features that made it useful in ranching. The raised **pommel**, or horn, was made to hold the **lariat**, or rope, for roping cattle or other animals. Mexican saddles served as the model for the Western saddle still used today.*

INDIAN TRADITIONS

A Pueblo Indian village.

Josefina looked forward to visiting her friend Mariana at the nearby Indian pueblo. In Spanish, the word *pueblo* means *village*. Pueblo Indians lived in adobe homes that were attached, apartment-house style. Each village had its own language or dialect, government, and traditions, but most Pueblo Indians made their living by farming, just as Josefina's family did.

Josefina saw Mariana only a few times a year. Sometimes Papá let Josefina go with him when he went to the pueblo to trade. Sometimes the whole

Montoya family visited the pueblo on Christmas Day or other special feast days. Josefina liked to watch the slow, dignified ceremonial dances that went on for hours to the steady beat of a drum. The Montoyas were honored to be guests of Mariana's family at the festive meal that followed the dances.

A Pueblo Indian girl like Mariana worked beside her mother, aunts, and grandmothers to learn about housekeeping, gardening, cooking, and pottery-making. Corn was important in the Pueblo diet, so Mariana spent several hours each day at the hard work of grinding dried corn into cornmeal.

Pueblo women grinding corn.

Mariana also learned to make pots from the red clay found in the New Mexico soil. First, Mariana and her grandmother dug clay from their favorite spot in the hills above the pueblo. Next, they soaked it in water and mixed sand into the clay. When the clay was ready, Mariana rolled coils of clay between her hands. Once, when Josefina visited, she showed Josefina how to shape the coils into a pot. Later, Mariana polished the pot with a smooth stone, painted it, and fired it, just as Pueblo women had done for hundreds of years.

Mariana and Josefina both wore soft leather moccasins. Early Mexican and Spanish settlers admired the comfortable and practical moccasins worn by Indians. They adopted the Indian tradition of making and wearing moccasins as part of their everyday clothing.

INDIAN TRADITIONS

Coil Pot

•

Moccasins

WATER JAR
This Pueblo water jar is wider in the middle to make it easier to carry water without spilling. It has a slight depression in the bottom so it can be balanced easily on top of the head.

COIL POT

*Mariana painted her pots with brushes
made from the long, spiky leaves
of the yucca plant.*

MATERIALS

Large sharp knife

Self-hardening clay *(preferably red, or Mexican, clay)*

Paper towels

Table knife *(optional)*

Fine sandpaper *(220-grit or finer)*

Artist's paintbrush *(optional)*

Acrylic paints *(optional; black, brown, and off-white are traditional)*

DIRECTIONS

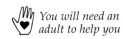 *You will need an
adult to help you*

1. Have an adult use the sharp knife to cut several pieces of clay. Each piece should fit into the palm of your hand.

2. Roll 1 of the pieces between the palms of your hands or on the table until it forms a rope about $1/4$ inch thick and 10 to 12 inches long.

3. Make several more clay ropes and set them aside. Cover them with damp paper towels to keep the clay soft.

Step 4

4. For the bottom of your pot, coil 1 clay rope into a tight spiral about 3 inches across. Dip your fingertips in water, and smooth the coiled clay by gently pinching and rubbing it with your damp fingers.

Step 5

5. After you have a base, start coiling the ropes up and slightly outward. When your pot is about 1 inch tall, gently pinch and smooth the coils together with dampened fingers. You can also use the dull edge of a table knife to smooth the surface.

6. Continue adding clay ropes to build up the sides until your pot is about 3 inches tall, pinching and scraping each new coil to form a smooth surface.

7. Work the pot into a globe shape by coiling the last ropes gently inward. Stop when you have an opening at the top that is a little wider than your thumb.

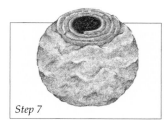

Step 7

8. Pinch around the mouth of the pot to form a smooth edge. Gently smooth and round out the whole pot. Dampening your fingers slightly may help. Leave a small flat area for the base, or bottom, of the pot.

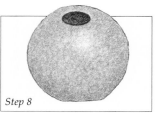

Step 8

9. Set your pot in a safe place, away from direct heat, and let it dry slowly for 2 or more days. Drying time depends on how dry or moist the air is. Every 8 or 10 hours, turn the pot gently so all sides are exposed to air. As it dries, the pot will shrink slightly. It is dry when it no longer feels cold to the touch.

10. After it is completely dry, use slightly damp sandpaper to carefully sand the surface. Wipe away the dust. If you want to decorate your pot, use an artist's paintbrush and acrylic paints. ✿

Step 10

23

MOCCASINS

Make a pair of soft, comfortable moccasins just like Josefina's.

MATERIALS

3 pieces of tracing paper
Pencil
Scissors
Straight pins
2 pieces of chamois leather, each about 18 inches square*
Fabric pen with disappearing ink
Leather spring punch*
Wax thread*
Needle with large eye

*Available at leather-supply stores. To find a leather store, look under
"Leather" or "Leather Supplies" in the yellow pages of the phone book.
Chamois can also be found in the automotive section of department stores.

DIRECTIONS

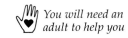 You will need an adult to help you

1. Use the tracing paper to trace the moccasin pattern pieces on pages 42 and 43.

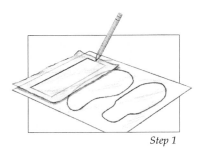
Step 1

2. The pattern is for size 1 shoes. If you need a different size, stand on the sole pattern and adjust the outline so there is 1 inch all around your foot. Cut out the sole. Increase or decrease the other 2 pattern pieces by the same amount, and cut them all out.

3. Pin the tracing paper patterns on your chamois and cut 2 of each pattern piece. Use the fabric pen to mark the X's and the Y's on all pieces, and the lace holes on the heel pieces.

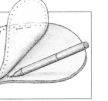
Step 3

4. Unpin your pattern pieces. Use the spring punch to punch small holes as shown on the pattern, 1/4 inch from the edge and 1/4 inch apart around the soles, the heels, and the *vamps*, or upper part of the moccasins.

Step 4

5. Lay the 2 soles on the table. Place a vamp on each sole, and line up the X's and Y's on the vamps with the X's and Y's on the soles.

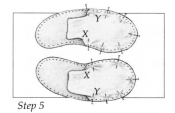
Step 5

6. Cut an 18-inch piece of wax thread, and then thread the needle. Tie a double knot at 1 end.

7. Starting at the X on the inside of the left moccasin, sew the vamp to the sole with a whipstitch. To whipstitch, come up at A. Stitch over the edge of the leather and come up at B.

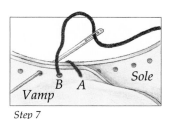
Step 7

8. When you reach the Y on the other side, line up the Y on the heel with the Y's on the sole and vamp. Your first few stitches will be through all 3 pieces, but the rest will be through just the heel and sole.

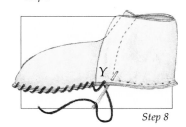
Step 8

9. Continue whipstitching all the way around the heel. The last few stitches will overlap all 3 pieces again. When you reach the X, knot the thread and cut off any extra thread.

10. Cut a tiny slit at each marked lace hole on the heel. To cut a slit, fold the chamois so the slit shows on the fold. Then cut a small slit on the line.

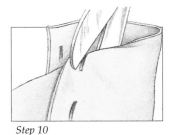
Step 10

11. Make laces from the extra chamois by cutting 2 pieces, each $\frac{1}{4}$ inch wide and 18 inches long. Thread the laces in the lace holes, and your moccasins are finished! ✽

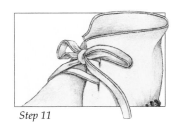
Step 11

A STITCH IN TIME

Josefina shared Mamá's thimble with her sisters when they sewed.

Evening was a special time on the rancho. Josefina and her family gathered near the fire in the family sala. There, they relaxed together—even though they continued to work. While they mended, sewed, and repaired tools, they talked about the day's activities, told stories, and teased each other with jokes and riddles.

In Josefina's time, girls learned to sew when they were very young. By the time they were five or six, Josefina and her sisters were learning to sew under Mamá's watchful eye. By the light of the fire,

Mamá had shown them first how to mend, and then how to make dresses, skirts, and *camisas,* or blouses. She had shown them how to cut fabric carefully, how to thread their needles, and how to sew everything together, stitch by tiny stitch.

Mamá also taught them *colcha*, a New Mexican style of embroidery Mamá had learned from her own mother. Colcha embroidery was used to decorate large bedcovers and church altar cloths. Colcha stitches varied in length and sometimes even crossed other stitches. That was because it was so often done by firelight, when it was hard to see. Josefina loved the beautiful and lively texture of colcha, but her stitching was never as skillful as Clara's!

Josefina's sisters learned how to weave on the large, upright loom in the weaving room. Josefina was too small to use the big loom, but she knew how to clean and spin the wool they used in making blankets and fringed sashes to wear with their skirts.

When Tía Dolores came to stay with them, she brought shiny new straight pins that Abuelito had bought from an *americano* trader in Santa Fe. Josefina decided she needed a special place to keep them. She turned a scrap of a fabric from one of Tía Dolores's dresses into a pincushion as plump as the pretty hen Señora Sánchez had given them!

A STITCH IN TIME

❋

Colcha Place Mat

•

Fringed Sash

•

Hen Pincushion

Women sometimes kept sewing diaries that held samples of fabric and notes about fashions.

COLCHA PLACE MAT

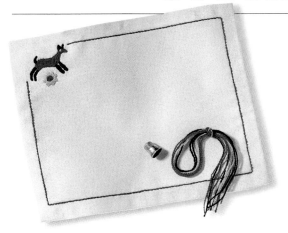

*Colcha embroidery uses two simple stitches—a short, single stitch and a longer one held down by smaller stitches called **couching** stitches.*

MATERIALS

Pencil and ballpoint pen

Piece of tracing paper, 5 inches square

1 place mat of open-weave cotton or linen *(off-white or white)*

Piece of fabric tracing paper, 5 inches square
(Dritz Mark-B-Gone is 1 brand.)

3-ply Persian wool or crewel wool yarn *(4 yards of red, 1 yard each of yellow and black)*

Scissors

Large-eyed embroidery needle

Ruler

DIRECTIONS

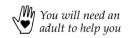 *You will need an adult to help you*

1. Use the pencil to trace the colcha pattern on page 42 onto the upper left corner of the tracing paper.

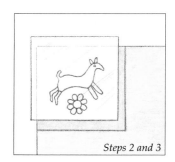

Steps 2 and 3

2. Lay the place mat flat on a table. Place the square of fabric tracing paper in the upper left corner.

3. Lay the sheet of tracing paper, design side up, on top of the fabric tracing paper.

4. Trace the pattern firmly with the ballpoint pen. Then remove both sheets of tracing paper. Your design will show on the place mat.

5. Cut a 2-foot piece of the yellow yarn. Separate 1 strand, or *ply*, of yarn from the rest, and thread your needle with the strand. Do not knot it—there are no knots in colcha embroidery.

6. Anchor the yarn by sewing 2 small running stitches inside the pattern. These stitches will be covered as you fill in the pattern. To sew a running stitch, go down at A and come up at B.

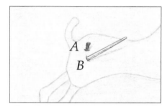

Step 6

7. Go down at C and come up at D, with the needle coming up at the edge of the pattern, near the deer's lower back leg.

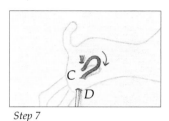

Step 7

8. Pull the yarn just enough to leave a short tail of yarn.

9. To sew a short colcha stitch, go down at A and come up at B, leaving only 1 or 2 place mat threads between your stitches. Cross over, and go down at C and come up at D.

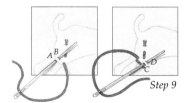

Step 9

10. Keep the yarn snug but not pulled tight or the stitches will pucker. Continue with short colcha stitches. If you miss a spot, go back and add stitches.

11. Vary the texture by using long stitches that are *couched,* or held down, by smaller stitches. First make a long stitch across the pattern, next to your last stitch, and go down at A. Then come up at B, halfway across the pattern. ➡️

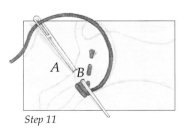

Step 11

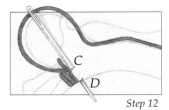

Step 12

12. Cross the long stitch *diagonally*, or at an angle, and go down at C. Come up again at D, at the far end. As you sew, you can change both where you start the couching stitch and its length.

Step 13

13. Keep stitching to fill in the pattern, using a combination of short and long stitches. Use different colors of yarn for the legs, ears, and tail. Step 13 shows the short and long colcha stitches.

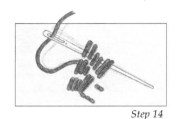

Step 14

14. When you reach the end of a piece of yarn, secure it by running it through the back of a few stitches on the back side of the fabric. The yarn will hold without knots.

15. Cut off the extra yarn. Then re-thread your needle and continue stitching.

IF AT FIRST YOU DON'T SUCCEED...

In Josefina's time, women and girls often did colcha embroidery in the evening, by firelight or candlelight. With so little light to sew by, they sometimes had to go back over their stitches in the morning and fill in spaces they had missed!

16. Finish the place mat by backstitching a border around it—except where you've embroidered your design—about 1 inch from the edge of the place mat. To backstitch, come up at A and go down at B.

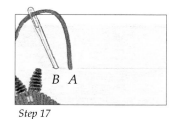

Step 17

17. Come up at C. Then go down at A and come up at D. Keep stitching all the way around.

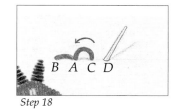

Step 18

18. When you're finished, secure the yarn by running it through the back of a few stitches on the back side of the fabric. Then cut off the extra yarn. ✽

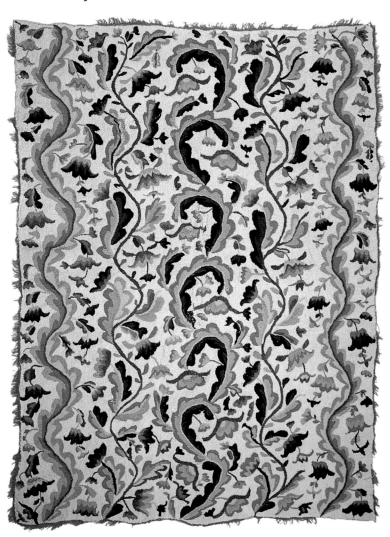

COLCHA EMBROIDERY

Women in Josefina's time used colcha embroidery to decorate large pieces such as bedcovers and coverings for church altars. Colcha stitches were easy to learn, fast to stitch, and used less yarn than other types of embroidery. The word **colcha** *also means "bed covering."*

FRINGED SASH

A fringed sash looks great with pants or a skirt.

MATERIALS

Loosely woven fabric, 2 yards long and
  7 inches wide *(lightweight wool, linen, or homespun)*
Straight pins
Ruler
Scissors
Thread to match the fabric
Needle
Iron

DIRECTIONS

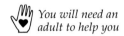 *You will need an adult to help you*

1. Fold the fabric in half lengthwise with the *right side,* or front side, facing in. Pin the edges together along the long side. Start pinning 6 inches from 1 end, and finish pinning 6 inches from the other end.

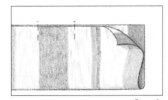
Step 1

2. Cut an 18-inch piece of thread, and then thread the needle. Tie a double knot at 1 end of the thread.

3. Starting 6 inches from 1 end, sew running stitches along the pinned side, $1/2$ inch from the edge. To sew running stitches, come up at A and go down at B.

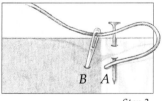
Step 3

4. Come up at C and go down at D. When you reach the end of your thread, tie a knot close to your last stitch and cut off the extra thread. Re-thread your needle and keep sewing until you are 6 inches from the other end. The 6 inches on the ends will become the fringes.

Step 4

5. Unpin the fabric, and turn the sash right side out. Have an adult help you iron the sash flat.

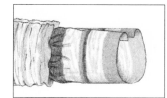

Step 5

6. To make a fringe on both ends of the sash, gently pull out the cross threads until you have fringes that are 6 inches long.

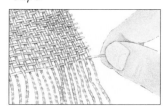

Step 6

7. Separate the threads into groups of 6 to 10 threads each.

8. For a simple fringe, tie each group in a knot close to the fabric.

Step 8

9. For a more elaborate fringe, braid the groups of threads, and then tie 2 or 3 braids together in a knot.

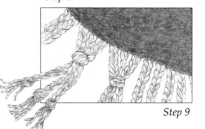

Step 9

10. Wrap the sash around the waist of your favorite skirt or pants, and knot it a little to the side.

FANCY FRINGES

Sashes can be fringed in many ways, both simple and elaborate. New Mexican women and girls liked to create interesting patterns and textures with the fringes of their sashes and shawls.

HEN PINCUSHION

*This plump, plucky hen makes
a perfect pincushion.*

MATERIALS

Pencil
Sheet of tracing paper
Scissors
Cotton fabric, 6 by 12 inches
Straight pins
Fabric pen
Thread
Needle
Ruler
Cotton balls
Felt scraps *(red, black, gold, and a color to match your fabric)*
Thick, tacky glue *(Aleene's Tacky Glue is 1 brand.)*

DIRECTIONS

1. Use the pencil to trace the patterns on page 42 onto the tracing paper. Cut out the patterns.

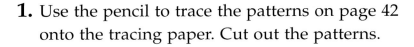

2. Fold the fabric in half, with the *right side*, or front side, facing in. Pin the body pattern to the fabric, and cut around the edges. Unpin the pattern, and pin the edges of the 2 pieces of fabric together.

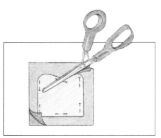

Step 2

3. On the wrong side of 1 piece, use the fabric pen to mark an X and Y on the fabric, as shown on the pattern.

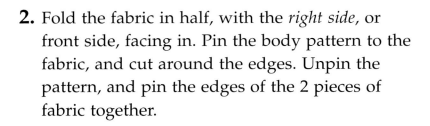

Step 3

4. Cut a 24-inch piece of thread, and thread the needle. Tie a double knot at the other end.

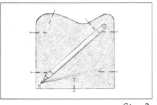

5. Backstitch the 2 pieces together, ¼ inch from the edge. Start at the X and go up toward the more rounded corner. To backstitch, come up at A and go down at B.

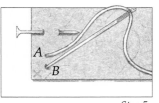

Step 5

6. Come up at C. Then go down at A and come up at D.

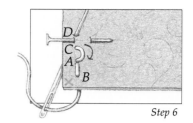

Step 6

7. Stitch until you reach the Y. Tie a knot close to your last stitch, and cut off the extra thread. Remove the pins, and turn the fabric so it is right side out.

8. Re-thread your needle so you have 18 inches of thread. Tie a double knot near the end.

9. Sew a running stitch all around the opening, ¼ inch from the edge. *Sew through 1 layer of fabric only*. Start at the Y, and stitch around the opening until you come back to the Y. To sew a running stitch, come up at A and go down at B. Come up at C and go down at D.

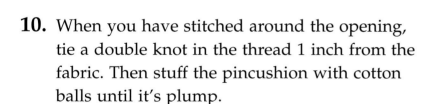

Step 9

10. When you have stitched around the opening, tie a double knot in the thread 1 inch from the fabric. Then stuff the pincushion with cotton balls until it's plump.

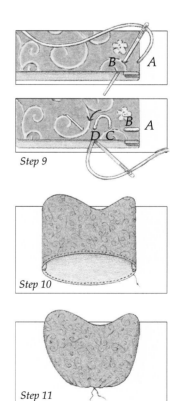

Step 10

11. Hold both double knots and pull the thread to *gather*, or pull together, the fabric. This closes the hole and makes a base for the pincushion. Tie the threads together in a double knot.

Step 11

12. Use the tracing paper patterns to make a felt beak, wattle, comb, wings, and tail feathers. Cut 2 tiny triangles for eyes. Then glue the pieces on. Cut a felt base and glue it to the bottom of the hen. ✳

FRONTIER FUN

*Girls like Josefina helped take care of
the younger children in a family.*

L ife on a busy rancho offered children little
time to play, but Josefina and her sisters knew
how to have fun while they worked. As they
did their daily chores, they sang songs, told stories
and riddles, and played guessing games. When
Josefina took care of Ana's little boys, she amused
them with *Tortitas* (Little Cakes), a Spanish game
similar to "Pat-a-cake," and other funny counting
games she played on their fingers and toes.

Children like Josefina learned to make toys and
playthings from the materials they found around the

rancho. They made whirlibirds from dried corncobs and feathers, and played Cat's Cradle with strands of the wool they used in weaving. They made tops from wood or clay, and used stones and beans for playing pieces in their games.

Josefina and her sisters spent sunny fall mornings in the courtyard husking corn. When they finished their work, Clara showed Josefina how to make dolls from the leftover cornhusks. They tied the dried husks together with twine made of twisted fibers from the yucca plant. Then they used glue they had made themselves to add dried corn silk for hair. Josefina was excited to have a new cornhusk doll to show her friend Mariana, who liked to play dolls as much as she did.

From the book *Meet Josefina*

Sometimes Josefina and her sisters had time for a lively game of *pon* after their morning chores. They spun a four-sided top on one of the large, flat stones in the courtyard, and used beans for counters. Francisca twirled the top as fast as she twirled her skirts when she danced! When the top landed with the T facing up, she yelled *"Todo!"* with such excitement that Tía Dolores came to see what all the noise was about. "Todo" meant that she had won all the counters in the basket. Francisca may have been the loudest, but Josefina was often the luckiest!

FRONTIER FUN

Cornhusk Doll

•

Pon Top and Game

HANDMADE TOYS

Not all handmade toys were as simple to make as cornhusk dolls. This hand-carved toy horse from the 1800s had movable joints.

37

CORNHUSK DOLL

When Josefina husked corn, she always saved some husks so she could make dolls.

MATERIALS

10 dried cornhusks*
Paper towels
Twine or 3 to 5 rubber bands *(tan or brown)*
Scissors
Corn silk or yarn for hair *(optional)*
White glue *(optional)*
Fine-point permanent felt-tip marker *(optional)*
*Available in craft stores and Mexican groceries.

DIRECTIONS

1. Soak the dried cornhusks in water for about 1 hour, to soften them. Pat them dry with paper towels.

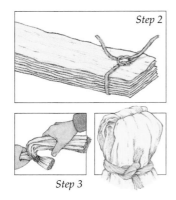
Step 2
Step 3

2. Make a pile of 8 husks. Tie twine or wrap a rubber band tightly around 1 end of the pile, about 1 inch from the end.

3. Separate the husks by holding 4 husks in each hand, and then pull the long ends apart and back over the twine or rubber band. Push the bunched end up with your thumb. Wrap twine or a rubber band around the ball that is formed. This is the head.

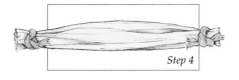
Step 4

4. Make arms by tightly rolling 2 husks together lengthwise. Wrap twine or rubber bands tightly near each end.

5. Slide the arms through the body, just below the neck.

6. Wrap and tie twine or a rubber band in a crisscross pattern across the doll's chest and under the arms. This will hold the arms in place.

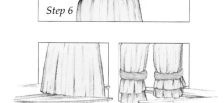

Step 6

7. Use the scissors to trim the bottom of the skirt evenly. Or, make legs by cutting 1 to 2 inches into the middle of the cornhusk skirt. Then wrap each leg at the ankle, and trim evenly.

Step 7

8. If you want to add hair, glue some corn silk or yarn to the top of the doll's head after the doll is completely dry. You can also draw a face on the doll with a felt-tipped marker. ✽

Step 8

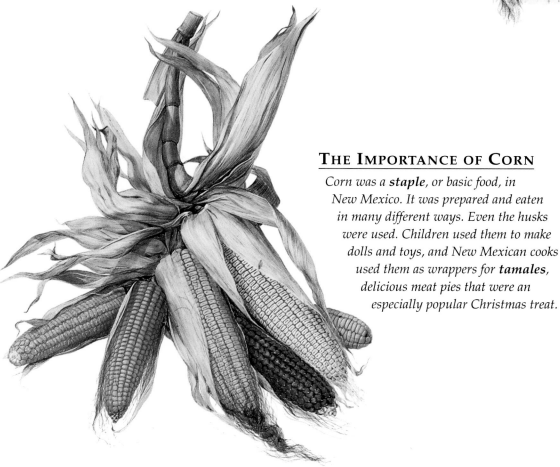

THE IMPORTANCE OF CORN

*Corn was a **staple**, or basic food, in New Mexico. It was prepared and eaten in many different ways. Even the husks were used. Children used them to make dolls and toys, and New Mexican cooks used them as wrappers for **tamales**, delicious meat pies that were an especially popular Christmas treat.*

PON TOP AND GAME

This clay top is simple to make.

MATERIALS

Large sharp knife
Self-hardening clay *(preferably red, or Mexican, clay)*
Ruler
Acrylic paints *(any color)*
Artist's paintbrush

DIRECTIONS

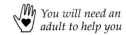 *You will need an adult to help you*

1. Have an adult use the knife to cut a piece of clay that will fit into the palm of your hand. Pinch off another piece of clay about the size of your thumbnail and set it aside to make a handle later. Roll the rest of the clay into a ball.

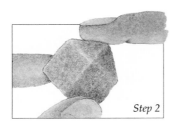
Step 2

2. Shape the ball into a 1-inch cube by flattening the sides and top. Then shape the bottom into a pyramid-shaped point (a point with 4 sides).

3. Make a handle by rolling the small piece of clay between the palms of your hands or on the table until it forms a clay rope about 1 inch long and 1/4 inch thick. Attach the handle to the top by working the clay pieces together with your fingers.

4. Put your top in a safe place, away from direct heat, to dry for 1 or 2 days. Drying time depends on how dry or moist the air is. Every 8 or 10 hours, gently turn it so all sides are exposed to air. As it dries, the top will shrink slightly. It is dry when it no longer feels cold to the touch.

5. When the clay is completely dry, use the artist's paintbrush to paint a letter on each side: P, S, N, and T. The letters stand for Spanish words that tell the actions of the game:

> **P** = *Pon*, or put in your counter(s)
> **S** = *Saca*, or take out your counter(s)
> **N**= *Nada*, or do nothing
> **T** = *Todo*, or you win the whole pot

Step 5

THE GAME OF PON (2 OR MORE PLAYERS)

1. To play, you need the top, a table, a small bowl, and pebbles, beans, or pennies to use as counters—enough for 6 counters per player.

2. Give 6 counters to each player. Each player puts 1 counter into the bowl.

3. To start, the first player says out loud how many counters she is willing to risk. Then she spins the top. If it lands with P facing up, she puts into the bowl as many counters as she risked. If it's S, she takes from the pot as many counters as she risked. If it's N, she does nothing, and the next player spins.

4. When a player gets T, she takes all the counters in the pot. Then all players—including the one who just won—must put in another counter to keep the game going.

5. If a player is out of counters, she's out of the game. The game ends when someone wins all the counters. ✳

TOPS

*Pon tops were probably modeled on the **dreidel** (DRAY-dl), a four-sided top used by Jewish people in Europe. Almost all Spanish and Mexican settlers in New Mexico were Catholic, but some had Jewish heritage. To protect their families, many Spanish Jews converted to Catholicism in the 1500s, a time of terrible persecution in Spain. By the time these families arrived in New Mexico, they had practiced Catholicism for generations, but they still held on to some Jewish customs.*

PATTERNS

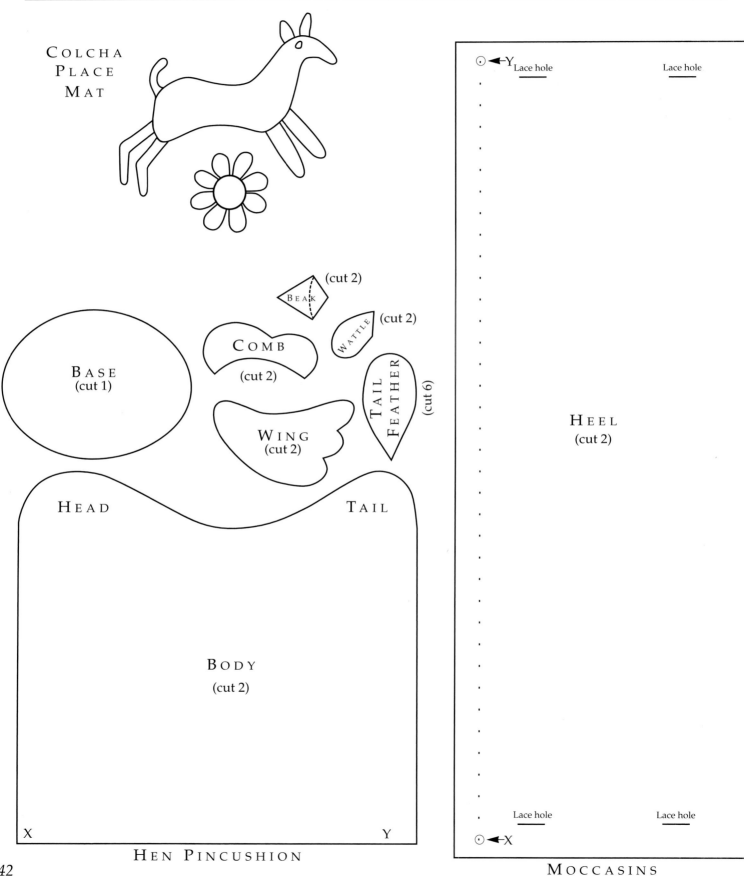

COLCHA
PLACE
MAT

BEAK (cut 2)

WATTLE (cut 2)

COMB (cut 2)

BASE (cut 1)

TAIL FEATHER (cut 6)

WING (cut 2)

HEAD   TAIL

BODY (cut 2)

X   Y

HEN PINCUSHION

Y → Lace hole   Lace hole

HEEL (cut 2)

Lace hole   Lace hole

X

MOCCASINS

APPLIQUÉD
TREASURE BOX

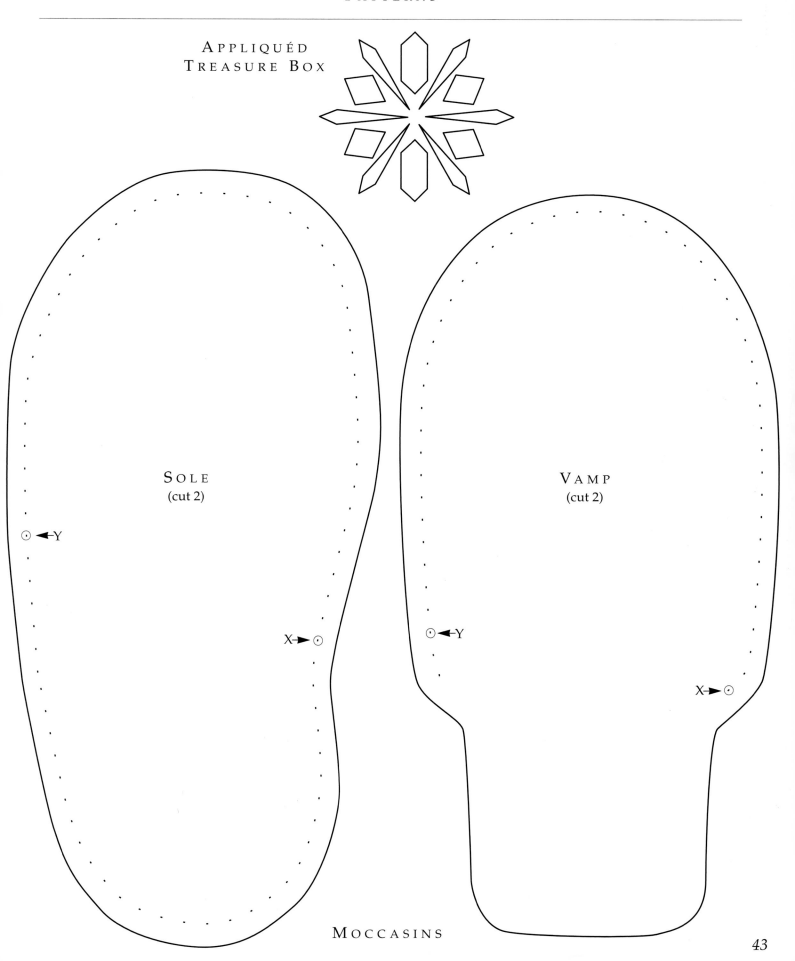

SOLE
(cut 2)

⊙ ◀—Y

X—▶ ⊙

VAMP
(cut 2)

⊙ ◀—Y

X—▶ ⊙

MOCCASINS

GLOSSARY OF SPANISH WORDS

BUILDING WITH ADOBE

*Most New Mexican houses were built by covering sun-dried **adobe** bricks with a coating of adobe, or mud, plaster. The plaster sealed the walls and kept moisture from damaging the building. Every spring, women and girls gave the walls of their homes a new coat of adobe plaster.*

BUILDING SANTA FE

Spanish and Mexican settlers started building New Mexico's capital city of Santa Fe in about 1608. Santa Fe is the oldest capital city in the United States.

Abuelito *(ah-bweh-LEE-toh)*—Grandpa

adobe *(ah-DOH-beh)*—a building material made of earth mixed with straw and water

araña *(ah-RAH-nyah)*—spider; also a spider-shaped wooden chandelier

Camino Real *(kah-MEE-no rey-AHL)*—the main road from Mexico City to New Mexico. Its name means "Royal Road."

camisa *(kah-MEE-sah)*—blouse

chile *(CHEE-leh)*—the fruit of a chile plant; also called "chile pepper"

colcha *(KOHL-chah)*—a kind of embroidery made with long, flat stitches

escoba *(es-KOH-bah)*—broom

escobetilla *(es-koh-beh-TEE-yah)*—small brush, or hairbrush

mantilla *(mahn-TEE-yah)*—a lacy scarf that girls and women wear over their head and shoulders

nada *(NAH-dah)*—nothing

niña *(NEE-nyah)*—girl

piñón *(pee-NYOHN)*—a kind of short, scrubby pine tree

pon *(pohn)*—a kind of spinning top; a game; also a command meaning "put in"

pueblo *(PWEH-blo)*—a village of Pueblo Indians

rancho *(RAHN-cho)*—a farm or ranch where crops are grown and animals are raised

saca *(SAH-kah)*—a command meaning "take out"

sala *(SAH-lah)*—a large room in a house

Santa Fe *(SAHN-tah FEH)*—the capital city of New Mexico. The words mean "Holy Faith."

señora *(seh-NYO-rah)*—a married woman; also a title, as "Mrs."

siesta *(see-ES-tah)*—a rest or nap taken in the afternoon

tamales *(tah-MAH-les)*—spicy meat surrounded by cornmeal dough and cooked in a cornhusk wrapper

tía *(TEE-ah)*—aunt

todo *(TOH-doh)*—all, everything

tortitas *(tor-TEE-tahs)*—small cakes